Moments With God

Turn Waiting Into Praying

Jacquelyn Graham

For God alone my soul waits in silence,
for my hope is from him.

PSALM 62:5

Liguori
ONE LIGUORI DRIVE
LIGUORI MO 63057-9999

Imprimi Potest:
Harry Grile, CSsR, Provincial
Denver Province, The Redemptorists

Published by Liguori Publications
Liguori, Missouri 63057

To order, call 800-325-9521, or visit liguori.org

Library of Congress Cataloging-in-Publication Data

Graham, Jacquelyn S.
 Moments with God : turn waiting into praying / Jacquelyn S. Graham.—1st ed.
    p. cm.
1. Mothers—Prayers and devotions. 2. Catholic women—Prayers and devotions.
I. Title.
 BV4847.G68 2012
 248.8'431—dc23

2012020775

p ISBN 978-0-7648-2214-8
e ISBN 978-0-7648-6734-7

Scripture quotations are from *New Revised Standard Version Bible*, copyright © 1989 National Council of the Churches of Christ in the United States of America. Used by permission. All rights reserved.

Liguori Publications, a nonprofit corporation, is an apostolate of The Redemptorists. To learn more about The Redemptorists, visit Redemptorists.com.

Printed in the United States of America
16 15 14 13 12 / 5 4 3 2 1
First Edition

Contents

Introduction

Have you ever found yourself getting impatient with the speed of the microwave? Or the copy machine? And then feeling ridiculous because of the absurdity of your dissatisfaction with these time savers?

Such has become the pace of our life that waiting four and a half minutes for our microwave lunch to cook or the fifteen seconds it takes for our original to be scanned and copied seems like a great inefficiency and a waste of our precious time.

Sometimes waiting is a mere annoyance, and sometimes it can be a source of great stress as we await the outcome of a particular situation—staring into the unknown, vacillating between hope and despair.

But waiting can be a gift—kind of a gift card that can be redeemed for the luxury of contemplation and the pleasure of prayer, a quiet conversation with God that can lower our blood pressure and heal our souls. While we anticipate the future, waiting keeps us in the present—in the presence of God.

This book is filled with prayers for those situations when we are forced to wait. These are times when we are not in control, because seldom do we choose to wait when we have the choice of moving on. Someone or something else is governing our life during that time.

When you find yourself waiting, look in the contents section at the beginning of this book for the situation that fits your life in that moment. Each devotion will begin with a prayer that will remind you of God's place in your life and focus your thoughts. A Scripture quotation and reflection follow. They contain wisdom to help you think beyond the obvious, to go deeper into the meaning of that moment in time. Then, in "A Moment With God," you will find questions and prayers that will enable you to spend a moment in prayer for your immediate needs and the needs that may have surfaced through your newly awakened awareness of your unity with all of God's works. You will end with a prayer called a "Collect" (emphasis on the first syllable), which gathers your thoughts and new discoveries and offers them to God. Of course, you have the freedom to adapt any of these prayers to your unique situation.

What a wonderful opportunity to grow in our understanding of our relationship with God! It is in our experiences of waiting that we can learn to give ourselves over to the one who loves us and waits with us.

Chapter 1
Children and Family

You show me the path of life.

Psalm 16:11

Waiting for Childbirth

Prayer

O God, you have made me a partner in bringing your precious gift of life into the world. Bless us both with your care and love. Calm my fears and fill me with peace as I await the birth of this child. Amen.

The Word of God

When Elizabeth heard Mary's greeting, the child leapt in her womb. And Elizabeth was filled with the Holy Spirit and exclaimed with a loud cry, "Blessed are you among women, and blessed is the fruit of your womb....
And blessed is she who believed that there would be a fulfillment of what was spoken to her by the Lord."

LUKE 1:41–42, 45

Reflection

Elizabeth and Mary were unlikely women to become mothers of two such extraordinary men. One was too old and thought to be barren; one was very young and had never been with a man. They both had doubts about their pregnancies.

During pregnancy it is not uncommon to have doubts about our suitability to be a mother or father of our first child or to be worried that we will have the energy and wisdom to skillfully bring this new child into our established family.

But this is no stranger leaping in your womb. As you await the birth of this child you can use this time to become well-acquainted, so that, when your time of fulfillment comes, it will be three old friends—Mom, Dad, and Baby—who join together in love to go forward into life.

A Moment With God

What fears or concerns do you have for this pregnancy?

Mary, Mother of God, pray for me that I may be blessed with good health as I carry this baby to a safe delivery.

What fears or concerns do you have for this impending birth?

Mary, Mother of God, with your tender care, watch over me and all those giving birth to new life.

What other prayers do you have at this time?

Prayer

Lord of life, you have blessed me with the gift of this child. Help me to fulfill my role as parent in a way that reflects your unconditional love for your children. I ask this through your Son, our Lord. Amen.

Waiting for the Baby to Wake Up

Prayer

O God, you have shown your patience with me all through my life. Help me to calm myself as I wait for ___N.___ to wake up so that we can complete the day's tasks and errands. Amen.

The Word of God

A gale arose on the lake, so great that the boat was being swamped by the waves; but [Jesus] was asleep.

MATTHEW 8:24

Reflection

There are days when you think it can't happen, but it does. Your child continues to sleep through the "gale" of your day. You need to run errands or leave for an appointment or family event. Do you wake him up and take a chance on being accompanied by a crying, unhappy child as you go about your rounds? Do you try to bundle her up while she's still sleeping and get her into the stroller or car without waking her up?

There are different answers to this dilemma every day and in every circumstance, but for now, use this time to reflect on the gift of this precious child, the gift of precious silence, and the gift of this break in your busy day.

A Moment With God

What are your hopes and dreams for this child who is sleeping so peacefully?

Lord, give me the wisdom and good judgment to make good decisions for my child and to guide ___N.___ well throughout her life.

Who are the people who might be waiting for you? What are the tasks that must wait while your child sleeps?

Lord, soften the hearts of the people who are dependent on me today. Help them and help me to order our priorities wisely.

When was the last time you longed for the peace and quiet that you are experiencing now?

Lord, I am listening intently. Into this silence speak to me your words of life.

What other prayers do you have at this time?

Prayer

O God, you are present in the silence and in the chaos of our daily living. Bless my family with a day that brings us the accomplishments we need to make, but never at the expense of the welfare of this child you have given us. I ask this through Christ our Lord. Amen.

Waiting for the Kids to Come Home From School

Prayer

O God our Father, you have given me these precious children who are tumbling back into my life after a day at school. Grant that I may welcome them and give them the attention they deserve in these few hours that we have together for the rest of this day. Amen.

The Word of God

If you love to listen you will gain knowledge,
and if you pay attention you will become wise.

SIRACH 6:33

Reflection

You may be waiting at home for the bus or carpool or waiting in your car for your children to come home from school. Either way, your surroundings are much quieter now than they will be soon, so you have time to prepare yourself mentally, emotionally, and spiritually to be present to your children in whatever way they need you to be. Their day may have been wonderfully successful, and your children may be filled with eagerness to tell you all about it. Or their day may have been filled with angst, with defeats, with failures. They may clam up or they may need to talk. Or one child may be up and one child may be down.

It takes the wisdom of Solomon, or Sirach, to know how to be what each child needs the most. Mistakes will be made, and your day may take on a note of failure. But if whatever you do, you do in love, in the selfless love of God, you will give your children what they need—to know that you are a safe haven in their world.

A Moment With God

What are the needs of each of your children? Hold each child up in prayer before the Lord.

Lord, bless _____N._____ . May he _____.

What kind of environment do you wish for your home during these next hours?

Lord, bless our family. Give us peace and harmony as we end this day in your loving care.

What other prayers do you have at this time?

Prayer

Loving God, you have blessed me with wonderful children to guide and nurture in your love. Give me a listening heart and the gifts of patience, wisdom, and understanding so that I may serve my children well. Make my words to them your words of love. I ask this through your Son, Jesus Christ our Lord. Amen.

Waiting to Pick Up the Kids
From Their Lessons and Classes

Prayer

Lord God, you watch with me as my children grow and develop their gifts and talents. May I have the grace to be their biggest cheerleader and the wisdom to have a healthy perspective so they'll learn what is really important for a life well lived. Amen.

The Word of God

When his parents saw him they were astonished; and his mother said to him, "Child, why have you treated us like this? Look, your father and I have been searching for you in great anxiety." He said to them, "Why were you searching for me? Did you not know that I must be in my Father's house?" But they did not understand what he said to them. Then he went down with them and came to Nazareth, and was obedient to them. His mother treasured all these things in her heart. And Jesus increased in wisdom and in years, and in divine and human favor.

Luke 2:48–52

Reflection

Mary and Joseph were as surprised as any parent when they realized that their Son Jesus was developing his own interests and goals. It is always amazing to us that this child who seemingly so recently was so dependent on us—who once thought we were the smartest people on the planet—now is pursuing interests that (perhaps) are a surprise to us. As parents, we want to give our children all the opportunities possible to help them grow and develop their gifts and talents. And as parents, we strive to guide our children in using those gifts and talents as a source for good in the world.

A Moment With God

Place your child's name before the Lord as he learns and grows in today's endeavor.

Lord, bless _____ N. _____ as he studies and practices _____.

Think about the children who, because of poverty or parental indifference, do not have the opportunities of your children.

Lord, give us a world in which all children can have the chance to live up to their potential.

What other prayers do you have at this time?

Prayer

Heavenly Father, all of our gifts and talents find their source in you. Guide my children, Lord, as they study and practice the arts they love, to use them in a way that will enrich and improve the world around them. Let them unselfishly share with others their abilities and "increase in wisdom and in years, and in divine and human favor," as did your Son, Jesus Christ our Lord. Amen.

Waiting for the Kids at Their Sports Practice

Prayer

O God, you have guided me in raising my child to pursue interests that will build strength and character. Bless _____N._____ , who is learning to compete well. Keep her safe and healthy in body and mind. Amen.

The Word of God

Train yourself in godliness, for, while physical training is
of some value, godliness is valuable in every way,
holding promise for both the present life and the life to
come. For to this end we toil and struggle, because we have
our hope set on the living God, who is the Savior
of all people, especially of those who believe.

1 Timothy 4:7b–8, 9–10

Reflection

Participation in sports, like so many activities in our lives and in the lives of our children, can be an exhibit of the worst of human nature or present us with an opportunity to be a force for good. The discipline of the game or the athletic activity builds character, teaches us about the dynamics of teamwork, and instills in us a sense of fairness, all of which will serve us well throughout our lives. If our children participate in a sport like tennis, wrestling, or track, they learn self-reliance and the joy of challenging themselves to constantly improve their skills.

Sports will develop these characteristics in players if they are coached and parented in a way that emphasizes strong Christian values, such as the Golden Rule: "Do unto others as you would have them do unto you," or, as was written in this Letter to Timothy, if they are also trained in "godliness."

A Moment With God

What are the qualities that you want your child to develop through this sport?

*Lord, through this sport may my child grow in _____.
Guide the coach in teaching these values to the children on this team.*

What are your fears for your child in this sport? Place them before the Lord.

Lord, I give my fears to you to help me bear. Give me the powers of observation that I need to make sure that my child is safe in body, mind, and spirit.

What other prayers do you have at this time?

Prayer

God of the living, you gave my child a body that has the potential to do great and wonderful things. Let me never lose sight of my need protect my child's body and to nourish his spirit. May my child learn to live in your ways, O Lord. I ask this through Jesus, your Son. Amen.

Waiting for Your Teenager
Who Has Missed Curfew

Prayer

Father in heaven, you gave me this child but did not guarantee that parenting would be easy. Bring my child safely home to my love and respect rather than my anger and anxiety. Amen.

The Word of God

Jesus told them this parable: "Which one of you, having a hundred sheep and losing one of them, does not leave the ninety-nine in the wilderness and go after the one that is lost until he finds it? When he has found it, he lays it on his shoulders and rejoices. And when he comes home, he calls together his friends and neighbors, saying to them, 'Rejoice with me, for I have found my sheep that was lost.'"

LUKE 15:3–6

Reflection

Right now you may be vacillating between worry and anger. These are legitimate emotions and worthy of being expressed. Your child may be in danger. Or your child may be thoughtless and irresponsible. There is no upside to this situation. She didn't call. He didn't text. You are justified in feeling this way. You are very busy right now preparing a speech your child will never forget.

But pause a moment. When your child walks through that door, in the midst of your anger and worry, you will be feeling the joy of the shepherd who has found the lost sheep. Don't hide that joy.

It is also a honest emotion. Worry, anger, joy. Your child needs to see all of these. And then you can listen to each other, speak the truth to each other, and love each other.

A Moment With God

Name your worries and place them before the Lord.

> *Lord, these are my fears:_____.*
> *Take them to yourself. Calm and comfort me.*

Pray for the well-being of your child as he journeys toward adulthood.

> *Lord, bless _____N._____ as he strains against the restrictions of childhood toward adult independence. Let my child never feel abandoned by you, Lord, or by me.*

What other prayers do you have at this time?

Prayer

> Shepherd God, your love is infinite and unconditional. Guide my words when my child arrives home. Endow me with your wisdom, honesty, and right judgment, but most of all help me to express the love I have for my child that causes these emotions to well up inside of me. I ask this through your Son, our Lord Jesus Christ. Amen.

Waiting for Your Child to Arrive Home From College

Prayer

God our Father, you have kept _____N._____ in your care as she has been away at college. Watch over and protect my child as she returns home and help us all to adjust to our changed family during this visit. Amen.

The Word of God

The beginning of wisdom is this: Get wisdom,
and whatever else you get, get insight.
Prize her highly, and she will exalt you;
she will honor you if you embrace her.
She will place on your head a fair garland;
she will bestow on you a beautiful crown.
Hear, my child, and accept my words,
that the years of your life may be many.
I have taught you the way of wisdom;
I have led you in the paths of uprightness.

Proverbs 4:7–11

Reflection

The child you sent to college a few months ago may be somewhat different from the person who will return to you today. Often the first visit home is the hardest. She has been living as an adult without curfews or a parent who knows where she goes and with whom. She has been exposed to new ideas and a diversity of people unknown to her in her high school experiences. You now have an independent young adult eagerly returning to a childhood home who will find herself chafing at your house rules.

Your young person has been accumulating wisdom. This is why you sent her to college. During this visit you must use the wisdom you possess. You have raised this person to be an upright human being. You must trust that, even when your beliefs and standards are being challenged, the foundation that you established is still there. With mutual respect and love, it will get easier.

A Moment With God

Consider and pray for what you want this visit to be.

Lord, let this time be one of peace that comes from respect and love for one another.

What behaviors do you want God to support in you?

Lord, remind me to listen to my child more than I speak. Other behaviors with which I will need help are

_____.

What other prayers do you have at this time?

Prayer

God of wisdom, you have opened up to my child a new world of knowledge and experiences. Inspire me to teach my child in the way of wisdom through the unconditional love we share for her. I ask this through Christ our Lord. Amen.

Waiting for Your Spouse to Arrive Home

Prayer

Lord God, you have blessed me with a partner in life and in love whom I treasure. Bring ___N.___ safely home to me (our family). Give us the gift of time with each other. Amen.

The Word of God

[Tobias and Sarah] began to pray and implore that they might be kept safe, Tobias began by saying, "Blessed are you, O God of our ancestors, and blessed is your name in all generations forever. Let the heavens and the whole creation bless you forever. You made Adam, and for him you made his wife Eve as a helper and support. From the two of them the human race has sprung. You said, 'It is not good that the man should be alone; let us make a helper for him like himself.' I now am taking this kinswoman of mine, not because of lust, but with sincerity. Grant that she and I may find mercy and that we may grow old together."

Tobit 8:4–7

Reflection

Tobias and Sarah had reason to be worried. Sarah was under a curse, and so far she had had seven husbands who had not survived their wedding night. This prayer that she and Tobias offered on this wedding night broke the curse, and they lived to a happy old age.

Sometimes in a marriage it seems as if we are under a curse. Things are not going right. We are not communicating. We are neglecting each other. The troubles of the outside world have come into our home and taken over.

Having the faith to place ourselves in God's mercy and care can go a long way toward breaking the curses that can grow in a relationship that takes for granted the gifts that we each bring to the other. Praying together can be a new form of not only communicating with God but with each other as well.

A Moment With God

Reflect on what you want for your marriage relationship.

Lord, give ____N.____ and me your gift(s) of
_____.

Ask God to bless your spouse and make you worthy of his/her love.

Lord, keep ____N.____ in your loving care and make me
worthy of our love by giving me the grace of _____.

What other prayers do you have at this time?

Prayer

God of love, in our marriage you have made us a part of your plan. Bless our relationship, and may our love model your unconditional love for your children to all who see us and know us. I ask this through Christ our Lord. Amen.

Waiting for a Call With Good (or Bad) News

Prayer

O God, you are present in my life day after day. Now I await a call that might contain good news or bad. When the call comes, Lord, sustain me in your love. Rejoice with me if the news is good. Grieve with me if the news is bad. Amen.

The Word of God

The spirit of the Lord God is upon me,
because the LORD has anointed me;
he has sent me to bring good news to the oppressed,
to bind up the broken-hearted,
to proclaim liberty to the captives,
and release to the prisoners;
to proclaim the year of the LORD's favor,
and the day of vengeance of our God;
to comfort all who mourn;
to provide for those who mourn in Zion—
to give them a garland instead of ashes,
the oil of gladness instead of mourning,
the mantle of praise instead of a faint spirit.

ISAIAH 61:1-3A

Reflection

When Jesus began his public ministry, he quoted these words from Isaiah in his hometown synagogue. At first people were impressed, but as he continued with his message that God belonged to all of humanity, not just Israel, the people grew angry and tried to kill him. As far as we know he never visited Nazareth again. These people were eager for the good news of Isaiah, but they couldn't accept what they considered the bad news of the universality of God.

God holds out the promise for us that what we see as bad news can become good news in the light of subsequent events. And the good news over which we rejoice can become bad news—the law of unintended consequences. Either way, we are dependent on God to bear us up in our lives, to give us "a garland instead of ashes."

A Moment With God

Hold up to the Lord all of the people who will be affected by this call if the news is bad.

Lord, give ___ N. ___ and ___ N. ___ the strength to overcome the adversity of this event.

Pray for all the people affected if the news is good.

Lord, help us to put good news into perspective.
Let not our good news hurt others.

What other prayers do you have at this time?

Prayer

Lord God, your Spirit continues to nourish me and inspire me to grow in my faith. Teach me, Lord, to grow beyond myself and embrace all who yearn for the Good News. I ask this through Christ our Lord. Amen.

Chapter 2
Household Tasks

One thing I asked of the LORD,
that will I seek after:
to live in the house of the LORD
all the days of my life.

PSALM 27:4

Waiting for Company to Come

Prayer

O God, who welcomes all who come to you, be with me as I welcome my guests into my home, as I make them comfortable, serve the meal, and guide the conversation. Help me to remember that when I welcome them, I welcome you. Amen.

The Word of God

Jesus said also to the one who had invited him, "When you give a luncheon or a dinner, do not invite your friends or your brothers or your relatives or rich neighbors, in case they may invite you in return, and you would be repaid. But when you give a banquet, invite the poor, the crippled, the lame, and the blind. And you will be blessed, because they cannot repay you. For you will be repaid at the resurrection of the righteous." One of the dinner guests, on hearing this, said to him, "Blessed is anyone who will eat bread in the kingdom of God."

LUKE 14:12–15

Reflection

The house is clean, dinner is prepared except for the last-minute tasks, the family has been oriented about proper behavior, and now it is simply a matter of waiting for your guests to show up. There's always a little stress because the evening before you has so many unknowns.

Rather than give handy hints for hosts, Jesus wants us to increase our stress by inviting not only people that we don't know, but people who are on the margins of society. People with whom we have nothing in common. The dinner guest got it. These people are blessed, as are we when we join them in the meal in God's kingdom. It is not just our homes that we must open to the lost and vulnerable, but our hearts. Now that's a party!

A Moment With God

Pray for the people in your community who are on the margins of society.

> *Lord, have mercy on all those who are homeless, poor, vulnerable or in distress.*

Pray for the people you will be hosting tonight who harbor pain and vulnerability you may not know about.

> *Lord, bless my guests tonight. May the hospitality I offer bring them comfort and peace.*

What other prayers do you have at this time?

Prayer

> Gracious God, you welcome all into your loving embrace. Increase my spirit of hospitality so that we may all eat bread together in the kingdom of God with Jesus, your Son, our Lord. Amen.

Waiting for the Coffee to Perk
or the Tea to Steep

Prayer

O God, you order my days and my nights. I thank you for
the time to enjoy this cup of coffee or tea I am preparing.
May it be a source of refreshment and renewal so that I may
be energized to continue my duties. Amen.

The Word of God

> *The LORD is my shepherd, I shall not want.*
> *He makes me lie down in green pastures;*
> *he leads me beside still waters;*
> *he restores my soul.*

PSALM 23:1–3

Reflection

In our American culture there is a work ethic that often insinu-
ates that rest is a waste of time. "How are you doing these days?"
"Oh, busy, busy, busy!"

To be busy is to be productive, and we think that to be productive means that we are of value to our community. We do not want
to admit that we are not busy. After all, "idle hands are the devil's
workshop." We even equate busyness with virtue.

The psalmist who wrote and sang the Twenty-Third Psalm
seems to be stating just the opposite. God wants to us to rest. He
used the metaphor of the shepherd who leads his sheep into green
pastures and still waters—no stress there. This shepherd God

doesn't suggest that we rest. He *makes* us lie down. It is only in rest that our souls can be restored.

So enjoy that cup of coffee or tea guilt-free. It is a gift from God.

A Moment With God

As you enjoy your cup, breathe in the aroma of your coffee or tea and thank God for the gift of creation that brought about your drink.

Lord, thank you for the coffee beans or tea leaves that enrich my day and bring joy to my palate.

Remember those who have grown and harvested your coffee or tea.

Lord, I hold up in prayer all those who have cultivated and harvested the coffee beans or tea leaves of this drink. May they be paid just wages for their work. May they farm in a way that sustains your gift of creation.

What other prayers do you have at this time?

Prayer

Creator God, you shepherd me throughout my day. May I always listen and attend to your commands with a heart that understands your love and concern for me. I ask this through your Son, Christ our Lord. Amen.

Waiting for Dinner to be Ready

Prayer

Lord, your bounty has no end. Bless us as we gather for this meal. May we always keep in mind those of your children who do not have enough food to sustain them. Amen.

The Word of God

On this mountain the LORD of hosts will make for all peoples
a feast of rich food, a feast of well-matured wines.
And he will destroy on this mountain
the shroud that is cast over all peoples,
the sheet that is spread over all nations;
he will swallow up death forever.
Then the LORD God will wipe away tears from all faces,
and the disgrace of his people he will take away
from all the earth,
for the LORD has spoken.

ISAIAH 25:6A, 7–8

Reflection

You are waiting for the promise of a meal to be satisfied. In Scripture, God used the meal as one of the ways he fulfilled his promise, whether it was to promise to deliver his Chosen People from their captors or to fulfill the promise of a Messiah who came to save us and in that process of salvation left us with a holy meal that 2,000 years later is still celebrated as Jesus celebrated it on the night before his death.

You may be the cook. You may be the guest or a family member. But as you prepare to sit down at table together for conversation and dining, reflect on the source of the gift of family, friends, eating companions, and the fruit of the land and seas before you. Take a moment to plan how you will give thanks and praise to God for these blessings.

Then reflect on those who are hungry and how you can share God's blessings with them.

A Moment With God

What promises has God fulfilled in your life? Bless God for his faithfulness.

Lord, I give you praise and thanks for all you have done for me.

Keep in mind those who find it difficult to put a meal on the table tonight.

Lord, wipe away the tears of those who are hungry. Open the hearts of your people that they may share their plenty with those who do not have enough.

What other prayers do you have at this time?

Prayer

Lord of hosts, you have placed before us the bounty of your goodness. Make us aware of those who are systematically excluded from the food you have provided for us all. Bring all peoples back to your table to share in your generosity. I ask this through your Son who fed the multitudes, Jesus Christ the Lord. Amen.

Waiting to Plant the Garden

Prayer

O Lord, you who created the heavens and the earth must appreciate how anxious I am to get out in the garden and begin planting. Bestow on me your gift of patience, Lord, so that when the soil is ready I will plant wisely and productively. Amen.

The Word of God

If you follow my statutes and keep my commandments and observe them faithfully, I will give you your rains in their season, and the land shall yield its produce, and the trees of the field shall yield their fruit. Your threshing shall overtake the vintage, and the vintage shall overtake the sowing; you shall eat your bread to the full, and live securely in your land. And I will grant peace in the land, and you shall lie down, and no one shall make you afraid.

LEVITICUS 26:3–6A

Reflection

Each year gardeners everywhere look forward to a new season in the persistent hope that this year will be the best ever! They endlessly debate with their fellow gardeners the best time to plant, the best methods to use, the best soil amendments to spread. Every detail is considered and reconsidered in the effort to achieve a lush, productive garden of vegetable and ornamental plantings.

When God made his covenant with Moses, God promised the Israelites fertile land, favorable weather, and generous harvests, all of which would lead to peaceful lives free from fear and danger. They only had to be faithful to God and the law.

The Israelites over their history broke their covenant with God, and things did not go so well for them. We have inherited those difficulties, but each spring we hold out hope for the promise of a good year, filled with the blessings of a fruitful harvest.

A Moment With God

Picture this year's garden and reflect on what you want to achieve there.

Lord, bless this year's garden. May it nourish the body and spirit of all who see it.

Hold up in prayer those whose lives are devoid of beauty and healthful food.

Lord, I pray for those who are hungry, homeless, victims of war and tyranny. Bring them relief from their sufferings.

What other prayers do you have at this time?

Prayer

Creator God, you have given this little piece of earth into my care. Bless my efforts as I plan my garden. Inspire me with your creative spirit so that all who enjoy my garden can share in your promise of peace and abundance. I ask this through Christ our Lord. Amen.

Waiting for Seeds to Sprout

Prayer

O God, in creating heaven and earth you planted seeds of all that is good and holy in our world. Bless the seeds I have put in this ground. Give me a productive harvest. Amen.

The Word of God

*Jesus said in a parable: "A sower went out to sow his seed;
and as he sowed, some fell on the path and was trampled
on, and the birds of the air ate it up. Some fell on the rock;
and as it grew up, it withered for lack of moisture.
Some fell among thorns, and the thorns grew with it
and choked it. Some fell into good soil, and when it grew,
it produced a hundredfold." As he said this, he called out,
"Let anyone with ears to hear listen!"*

LUKE 8:4–8

Reflection

Gardeners understand parables and metaphor. This fact is evidence that Jesus' disciples were not gardeners or farmers. They needed an explanation of this parable. Maybe it's the long hours alone in the garden planting, watering, pulling weeds, and managing pests that cause the mind to wander and the imagination to flower.

Jesus' explanation of the situations into which the seeds of the word of God are sown equates the path with the shallowness of mind that allows the devil to take away the seed, the rock with people who forget the word when they are tested by life's problems, the thorns with the distractions of life, and the good soil with those who hold the word in an "honest and good heart."

We, too, sow the seeds of faithfulness in everyone we touch. We, too, do not know what kind of harvest our seed will produce. But we are gardeners. We are optimists, and we will continue to plant, always.

A Moment With God

Pray for those to whom you would like to pass on your faith.

Lord, may my children, grandchildren, and friends be fertile ground for your word.

Pray for farmers and gardeners who are now sowing for this growing season.

Lord, grant those who grow our food good weather and a bountiful harvest.

What other prayers do you have at this time?

Prayer

Creator God, you know what it is to plant seeds that do not germinate in the way that you intended. As I await the sprouting of my seeds, keep me mindful that the important seeds I plant are the seeds of faith that will bring people to your Son, Christ our Lord. Amen.

Waiting for Fruit to Ripen
and Vegetables to be Ready to Pick

Prayer

Lord God, you know the care and love I have put into this ground and these plantings. Teach me patience as I await the right time to harvest all of the fruits of my labor. Amen.

The Word of God

Then I looked, and there was a white cloud, and seated on the cloud was one like the Son of Man, with a golden crown on his head, and a sharp sickle in his hand! Another angel came out of the temple, calling with a loud voice to the one who sat on the cloud, "Use your sickle and reap, for the hour to reap has come, because the harvest of the earth is fully ripe." So the one who sat on the cloud swung his sickle over the earth, and the earth was reaped.

REVELATION 14:14–16

Reflection

Eons ago, God planted the seeds that would become life on this planet today and in the future. God has cultivated and nourished our earth and we her fruits, even to the point of sending his Son to save us by his healings, his teachings, and his ultimate sacrifice. It is through Jesus Christ that we can exist in harmony with one another and our earth until it is time for the final harvest.

If you want an example of patience, look no further than the Great Gardener, who has had so many opportunities to pull us right out of the ground and toss us into eternal compost but who hasn't. Just as God is waiting for humankind to reach that perfection of ripeness that makes us worthy of the great banquet to be celebrated in the new Jerusalem, so must we wait patiently for the perfect ripeness in our own gardens so that we can grace our family and friends with the fruits of our harvest.

A Moment With God

Pray for those you will feed with your garden produce.

Lord, bless my family and friends and all who will benefit from the produce of my garden. Make my efforts worthy of these people I love.

Pray for those who do not have fresh food.

Lord, bless those who are hungry. Help me find a way to share my bounty with them.

What other prayers do you have at this time?

Prayer

God of the harvest, you have patiently cultivated me and nourished me with your love. May I make my life fruitful so that when the day comes I may be worthy of being a part of your bountiful harvest. I ask this through Jesus Christ our Lord. Amen.

Chapter 3
At Work

For the word of the LORD is upright,
and all his work is done
in faithfulness.

PSALM 33:4

Waiting for a Job Interview

Prayer

Lord God, you have answered my prayers through the granting of this interview. Be with me now. Help me to relax, to be at my best, and to answer questions in a way that will reflect favorably on me. Amen.

The Word of God

[Jesus said:] "You are the salt of the earth; but if salt has lost its taste, how can its saltiness be restored? It is no longer good for anything, but is thrown out and trampled under foot. "You are the light of the world. A city built on a hill cannot be hidden. No one after lighting a lamp puts it under the bushel basket, but on the lampstand, and it gives light to all in the house. In the same way, let your light shine before others, so that they may see your good works and give glory to your Father in heaven."

MATTHEW 5:13–16

Reflection

You have prepared for this interview conscientiously. You are dressed to reflect your respect for the interviewer and the position. You have done your research on the company and its place in the business world. And here you are. Nervous? Of course.

Jesus has some good advice: Be the salt of the earth. Give flavor to what you do and to all you meet. You are an interesting, engaging person. Don't hide that. Be yourself.

Be a light to the world. Don't hide your talents, your good qualities and your good works out of a sense of modesty. Even the most humble saints of God shone brightly to all they met. You can and should do the same.

God made you in God's own image. Never forget that, and never try to inhibit God's image from shining out in you. You are a child of God.

A Moment With God

Ask God to guide your thoughts and words today. Pray this centering prayer.

Lord, fill my mind with wisdom, my mouth with well-formed words and my heart with warmth that I may reflect your image.

Pray for your interviewer.

Lord, give your gift of discernment to my interviewer during this selection process.

What other prayers do you have at this time?

Prayer

Creator God, you have made me in your image and likeness. Keep me mindful of our blessed and grace-filled relationship as I sit for this interview. I ask for success, Lord, but if success is not to be found here, I humbly ask that I soon may be salt and light in another place. I ask this in the name of your Son, Jesus Christ the Lord. Amen.

Waiting for the Copy Machine

Prayer

Lord Jesus, you are the Word of God sent down from heaven. As I wait while these pages are being copied, instill in me an appreciation for the great responsibility it is to disseminate words, given the power that they carry. Amen.

The Word of God

Moses came and told the people all the words of the Lord and all the ordinances; and all the people answered with one voice, and said, "All the words that the LORD has spoken we will do." And Moses wrote down all the words of the LORD.

Exodus 24:3–4a

Reflection

Why are you standing here watching this copy machine spit out your copies? Well, because if you left, you know what would happen. A paper jam. Or the pink paper someone carelessly left in the feeder would infiltrate your copy job. So you stay and watch.

We often find ourselves reflecting on the monks who painstakingly copied the Bible and other books by hand, letter by letter. Words and the power to convey the thoughts they expressed were taken very seriously, perhaps because of the time-consuming effort it took to get them into the hands of those who would read them.

When Moses "wrote down all the words of the Lord," the covenant God made with Israel, part of which were the Ten Commandments, did he imagine that 6,000 years later these words would form the consciences of the people of two of the world's great religions?

A Moment With God

Who will be gathering information from these copies? Pray for a suitable outcome.

Lord, may this information be life-giving to those who are affected by it.

There are people in our world for whom words on a page are sense-less scratchings because they cannot read. What are their needs?

Lord, make me aware of those who lack literacy in my community and our world and show me how to be a part of the solution.

What other prayers do you have at this time?

Prayer

God of all, you have authority over all and in all. Bless me with wisdom as I place my thoughts and words before those with whom I work. Never let me forget the power of my words and the responsibility to use them well. I ask this through Christ our Lord. Amen.

Waiting for the Computer to Boot Up

Prayer

O God, you are present in the quiet of this time before my work can begin. Keep me mindful of your presence as I plunge into the busyness of this day. Help me focus on the tasks before me. Amen.

The Word of God

The LORD is good to those who wait for him,
to the soul that seeks him.
It is good that one should wait quietly
for the salvation of the LORD.
It is good for one to bear
the yoke in youth,
to sit alone in silence
when the LORD has imposed it.

LAMENTATIONS 3:25–28

Reflection

Often we see the time it takes for our computer to boot up as dead time, but when we can use it as a prayer time before our work obligations engulf us, it takes on such a value that we can actually be grateful for technology that is not immediately responsive to our needs. This chance to be quiet can be an invitation to bring the Lord into your day, to focus on the first few tasks at hand and to ask the Lord to guide your hands and mind for the good of all as you work and as you engage with others.

Perhaps it is not the Lord who has imposed silence upon you as wrote the author in the Book of Lamentations. It is your computer that has imposed this silence upon you. Praise God for the gift of this technology that allows you a moment of respite to put yourself in God's presence during this busy day.

A Moment With God

Pray for the people who have sent the e-mails that are waiting for you to open.

Lord, be present in my inmost thoughts so that I can answer my mail with wisdom and fairness.

Think about the use to which your computer will be put today.

Lord, guide my use of the programs I need and of the Internet today so that I can work efficiently and accurately.

What other prayers do you have at this time?

Prayer

Almighty God, you are present with me in this silence. Attend me on this day as I go about my tasks and as I interact with my coworkers both near and far. Give me a day that I can reflect upon with satisfaction at its close. I ask this through your Son, Jesus Christ our Lord. Amen.

Waiting for Your Next Work Assignment

Prayer

O God, you have given us the mission of doing your work here on earth. When I begin my next task, help me focus so that I can work efficiently and conscientiously and give a fair day's labor for my wages. Amen.

The Word of God

I [Paul] commend you to God and to the message of his grace, a message that is able to build you up and to give you the inheritance among all who are sanctified. I coveted no one's silver or gold or clothing. You know for yourselves that I worked with my own hands to support myself and my companions. In all this I have given you an example that by such work we must support the weak, remembering the words of the Lord Jesus, for he himself said, "it is more blessed to give than to receive."

Acts 20:32–35

Reflection

Idleness is difficult for people in our American culture. We want to keep busy at all costs. That is why we get impatient when we have to wait for our next assignment. Work has dignity. Even the Apostle Paul expressed his pride in being self-supporting.

But this is a good time to reflect on the value of our work. Does our work make life better or easier for someone? Jesus told us that is it "more blessed to give than to receive." Is our work an act of generosity rather than a self-serving act? If the answer to either of these questions is "no," then it might be a time to see what we have in our power to change. Is it really the nature of your work? Might an attitude adjustment be in order or is it just a lack of imagination? These are questions that can fill this time.

A Moment With God

Are there working relationships at your workplace that are problematic for you?

Lord, give me the grace to forge connections with ___N.___ that will enable us to work together in a more productive way.

Do you like your job? If not, what are your dreams?

Lord, sustain me as I work to realize my goals and aspirations.

What other prayers do you have at this time?

Prayer

Lord God, your work of creation is ongoing, and you never tire of bestowing all that is good on your people. Inspire me to act with respect toward others and give me a positive attitude so that I may be productive in my work as you have been productive in my life. I ask this through your Son, Jesus Christ our Lord. Amen.

Waiting for Your Lunch Break

Prayer

O God, you have watched over me as I have labored at my job during this morning. As I come to the end of this period of work and look forward to a relaxing meal, I give you my thanks for the work you have given me and for the meal that I will eat. Amen.

The Word of God

The disciples were urging [Jesus], "Rabbi, eat something." But he said to them, "I have food to eat that you do not know about." So the disciples said to one another, "Surely no one has brought him something to eat?" Jesus said to them, "My food is to do the will of him who sent me and to complete his work. Do you not say, 'Four months more, then comes the harvest?' But I tell you, look around you, and see how the fields are ripe for harvesting."

JOHN 4:31–35

Reflection

Before you take this break from work to eat, perhaps alone or perhaps with your coworkers, it is worthwhile to reflect of this passage from the Gospel of John. It seems here that Jesus did not think that it was important to eat. He was more interested in doing the work that his Father had sent him to do.

But the gospels are full of stories of Jesus' meals even after he rose from the dead. He thought that it was important to eat, it's just that it wasn't important what he ate as much as it was with whom he ate. He was in the habit of eating with people who are on the margins of Jewish life: tax collectors and sinners. This was very upsetting to the Temple hierarchy, but this was where Jesus' work was, his place of business, his factory floor.

A Moment With God

Who are the people who will be eating with you or who could be eating with you if you let them in? Hold them up in prayer.

Lord, bless my eating companions. May I follow your model of being present to them so as to assist in the work of your Father.

Think about your needs for the second half of the day. Place them before the Lord.

Lord, be with me in my work. May I accomplish my tasks as your servant.

What other prayers do you have at this time?

Prayer

Lord of the harvest, your work of the kingdom never ends. As I eat my lunch and continue my workday, feed me with the knowledge that as I nurture relationships with my co-workers, I must do so in a way that continues the work that you have sent me to do as you sent your Son, Jesus Christ our Lord. Amen.

Waiting for the End of Your Shift or the Close of the Day

Prayer

Lord, you have given me this day, the good and the bad of it. I thank you for all the moments of this day, with its lessons and its joys. May I leave my work behind and find rest with my friends and family. Amen.

The Word of God

Good things and bad, life and death, poverty and wealth, come from the Lord. The Lord's gift remains with the devout, and his favor brings lasting success. One becomes rich through diligence and self-denial, and the reward allotted to him is this: when he says, "I have found rest, and now I shall feast on my goods!" he does not know how long it will be until he leaves them to others and dies.

SIRACH 11:14–19

Reflection

If you have a little down time at the end of your work shift, spend it reflecting back on your day. What were the lessons that you took from your successes? Deadlines made, quotas reached, tasks accomplished, a relationship with a coworker improved. What were the lessons that you took from your failures? Can you come back tomorrow with this new knowledge and apply what you learned today? Every day is different, and everyone experiences each day differently.

Whatever you have experienced and learned today, one thing is certain. It was all a gift from God, a gift to be savored in contemplation as you make your journey home.

You have earned a rest. The rewards that you will be allotted and the goods upon which you will feast in gratitude will be the wisdom you have gained from God's gift of this day.

A Moment With God

Reflect on an event today that you would like to place before the Lord.

> *Lord, I place before you the time today when _____.*
> *I give you thanks for that event and all that it taught me.*

Pray for your coworkers.

> *Lord, bless those with whom I work. Inspire us to create and*
> *maintain an environment of cooperation, collaboration,*
> *and respect.*

What other prayers do you have at this time?

Prayer

> Lord God, in my work today you have shared with me your work of creation. Help me to remember the lessons of today so that my tomorrow may be even more productive and creative. Bless my coworkers and keep us all safe so that we may all return tomorrow to work together in harmony with one another. I ask this through your Son, our Lord. Amen.

Waiting for a Decision From the Boss

Prayer

Lord God, you are the highest authority in my life. Support and sustain me as I await this decision from my boss. Amen.

The Word of God

If God is for us, who is against us? He who did not withhold his own Son, but gave him up for all of us, will he not with him also give us everything else? Who will bring any charge against God's elect? It is God who justifies. Who is to condemn? It is Christ Jesus, who died, yes, who was raised, who is at the right hand of God, who indeed intercedes for us.

ROMANS 8:31B–34

Reflection

You have done your best work, you have made your presentation, stated your case and now it is out of your hands. The decision that your employer makes may impact the future of the company, your job, the jobs of your coworkers, your customers or even your own employment. You feel helpless and isolated from the process. To make matters worse, this scenario may not be its first time. It may have repeated itself many times over the course of your career.

Saint Paul was writing to people whose very lives were in danger from the Roman authorities. But his words help to put everything in perspective when we are feeling that helplessness and lack of control. It was for us that God made the ultimate sacrifice of his Son, and God will not let us down now. The answer may not be what we expect or even what we want, but in the answer, God is there. He will walk with us and uphold us in our trials. What we have in God's presence is what we need to endure this situation and any other situation in our lives.

A Moment With God

Hold up your boss in prayer.

Lord, give ___N.___ the wisdom and judgment to make the right decision for this company, its employees, and customers.

Pray for all who might be affected by this decision.

Lord, may this decision be sound and just for all who are affected by it.

What other prayers do you have at this time?

Prayer

Almighty God and king, your presence sustains me in these anxious times. Whatever this decision is to be, help me to graciously accept it and work with it. I ask this in the name of your Son, Jesus Christ, who intercedes for us before your heavenly throne. Amen.

Waiting for Customers

Prayer

O God, you know my heart and its anxieties and cares. Send me customers so that I can do my job and earn my wages. Guide me to present this product successfully. Amen.

The Word of God

Praise the LORD!
Happy are those who fear the Lord,
who greatly delight in his commandments.
They rise in the darkness as a light for the upright;
they are gracious, merciful and righteous.
It is well with those who deal generously and lend,
who conduct their affairs with justice.
For the righteous will never be moved;
they will be remembered forever.
They are not afraid of evil tidings;
their hearts are firm, secure in the Lord.

PSALM 112:1, 4–7

Reflection

How often are we pressured in our jobs to do things that make us uncomfortable, to be less than honest, or outright dishonest, to the people we deal with, to treat people not as we would want to be treated? Situations like this weigh on us heavily as we struggle to make a living and meet our responsibilities.

It is times like this that we must have that talk with God. Who doesn't want to be "gracious, merciful, and righteous?" How can we be true to our hearts under these circumstances? It is possible if we listen to God carefully. Company culture can be changed, and customers can be served with justice. And they will respond with loyalty.

In all situations, under all circumstances, let God guide you in how to treat people.

A Moment With God

Hold up your company and the people who work with you in prayer.

Lord, bless all who work here and inspire in the culture of this company a sense of integrity and right behavior.

Pray for your customers.

Lord, my customers will all come from different places in their lives. Allow me to make a difference to them as we deal with each other.

What other prayers do you have at this time?

Prayer

Lord God, you gave us the Golden Rule of treating others as we would like to be treated. I thank you for putting me in this place and time where I can be a part of your call to justice for all. Bless and guide my work. I pray this in Jesus' name. Amen.

Chapter 4
Out and About

I wait for the LORD, my soul waits,
and in his word I hope.

PSALM 130:5

Waiting to Get Past an Accident Scene

Prayer

O God, who watches over all things, give me patience and compassion as the human drama up ahead is unfolding. Help me in my own vulnerability as I pray for others. Amen.

The Word of God

Listen, I will tell you a mystery! We will not all die, but we will all be changed, in a moment, in the twinkling of an eye, at the last trumpet. For the trumpet will sound, and the dead will be raised imperishable, and we will be changed. For this perishable body must put on imperishability, and this mortal body must put on immortality.

1 Corinthians 15:51–53

Reflection

Any accident can serve to remind us that life can change in a "twinkling of an eye." We can never be ready for an accident. That's why it's called an "accident." But we can prepare ourselves for its aftermath by putting ourselves in God's care, submitting ourselves to God's love.

Waiting in the traffic jam caused by an accident fills us with conflicting emotions: anxiety and impatience to get to our destination, curiosity about what has happened and what we will witness when we get to the scene, sympathy for the people involved, and a feeling of "there, but for the grace of God, go I."

Moments With God

A Moment With God

If you were the victim of this accident, what kind of prayers would you want from those who pass by?

Lord, be present to these people in their difficulties and give them strength to face the consequences of this accident.

What do you want to pray for the emergency responders on the scene?

Lord, instill upon the drivers in the cars around me your patience and calming peace so that those who are assisting the victims of this accident may do so in safety.

What other prayers do you have at this time?

Prayer

Immortal God, you are the constant in an unpredictable world. Guide us, protect us, and make your love known to us when we meet the unexpected. We ask this through Christ our Lord. Amen.

Waiting for the Bus or Train

Prayer

O God, you have guided our ingenuity to create ways of transporting people to their destinations with precision and orderliness. Be with me in my comings and my goings among your people today. Amen.

The Word of God

O LORD, you have searched me and known me.
You know when I sit down and when I rise up;
you discern my thoughts from far away.
You search out my path and my lying down,
and are acquainted with all my ways.

PSALM 139:1–3

Reflection

As you wait for your bus or train to arrive and take you to your destination—be it work, shopping, an entertainment or sporting event, an evening with friends or family, or back home again—you have an opportunity to observe and give thanks for the diversity of the human race as created by God.

Reflect on the fact that with all of our differences we are all fellow travelers on this journey through our days and nights. How are you going to relate to your companions as you travel through the streets or on the rails? A smile, an act of kindness or courtesy, a showing of respect—just one of these actions can make another person's day, and all of them together just might make a life better. What is your next move?

Moments With God

A Moment With God

Each person is a story. Choose a person around you, respectfully observe him and make him a part of God's story for you by praying for that person.

Lord, I ask that you make your presence known in the life of this child of God. You know the needs of this person as no one else ever can. Bless and keep him in your care.

As each journey begins, we face many unknowns. What is ahead for you on this day?

Lord, walk with me through this day. Help me to make wise decisions and to be a blessing to all I meet.

What other prayers do you have at this time?

Prayer

Lord God, you know my needs and the needs of all those around me. Be with us as we face the joy and sorrows, the victories and defeats in each of our lives. Help us find the blessings you have placed before us on this day. We ask this through Christ our Lord. Amen.

Waiting at the Laundromat

Prayer

O Lord, as I sit in enforced idleness waiting for these clothes to be washed and dried, my thoughts turn to you and to the blessing of the clothes we wear, the sheets we sleep on, the towels we use in washing, and the technology that allows me to quickly and efficiently clean them. Receive my thanks for these your gifts as I wait, O Lord. Amen.

The Word of God

[Jesus said,] "Consider the lilies, how they grow: they neither toil nor spin; yet I tell you, even Solomon in all his glory was not clothed like one of these. But if God so clothes the grass of the field, which is alive today and tomorrow is thrown into the oven, how much more will he clothe you— you of little faith! And do not keep striving for what you are to eat and what you are to drink, and do not keep worrying.

LUKE 12:27–29

Reflection

Sometimes it is in those chores we would rather not have to do that God's dominion over us becomes clear. Reflect on how it came to be that you were born into a time, a place, and a culture that allows you to sit in a not-too-unpleasant spot while your washing is being done. Or how it came to be that you have the luxury of clean clothes, or the opportunity to bathe with those towels, of sheets for your bed, or even of a bed. In many parts of the world and even in our own country that expectation does not exist.

We are so blessed, yet even in our abundance we worry about having clothing that is stylish, towels that match, and sheets with the right number of threads per inch. Why?

A Moment With God

What are the true blessings in your life?

Lord, I thank you for these good things you have given me: (name them.)

What do you tend to worry about that you can let go and let God take care of?

Lord, I hand over my anxieties to you and ask for peace in my mind and in my soul.

What other prayers do you have at this time?

Prayer

Generous God, you have made me one of your lilies and have blessed me with all that is good in my life. Do not allow me to take your benevolence for granted or let me hold my material blessings so close that I forget those who are in need, who have never known the abundance that I enjoy. I ask this through Christ our Lord. Amen.

Waiting for an Appointment

Prayer

O God, you know my life: my past, my present, and my future. As I sit in this waiting room immersed in thoughts of my purpose here today, calm me so that I can express myself clearly and listen intently. May the outcome of this appointment have a positive impact on my life and the lives of those I touch. Amen.

The Word of God

Do not worry about anything, but in everything by prayer and supplication with thanksgiving let your requests be made known to God. And the peace of God, which surpasses all understanding, will guard your hearts and your minds in Christ Jesus.

PHILIPPIANS 4:6–7

Reflection

You may be waiting for an appointment with a doctor, a lawyer, an accountant, your boss, or any of the numerous people who have an impact on your life. You may expect that it will turn out very well or very badly, but one thing you do know is to expect the unexpected. It is times like these when we learn how little we are in control of our lives and our futures, even when we live our lives the best we can according to God's holy word. The only thing we can control is our own reaction to the events of our lives. Knowing that God is present in your life, walking beside you or sitting right there next to you, can give you the peace that will help you overcome your anxiety.

A Moment With God

What are the possible outcomes that you expect or desire from this meeting?

Lord, let the results my meeting with ___N.___ be according to your holy will.

How do you want your demeanor to present itself at this meeting?

Lord, may your presence to me manifest itself in my presence to ___N.___. Open my heart to all that is said and put your words on my lips.

Are there other people in the waiting room with you? What about the person or people with whom you are meeting?

Lord, bless these people with your peace as they go to their meetings. May all of the outcomes be according to your will.

What other prayers do you have at this time?

Prayer

Lord God, ruler of life, your presence upholds me in uncertain times. Stay by me in my encounter with ___N.___. Keep us both in your care, and bring us to an understanding of each other and our needs. I ask this through Christ our Lord. Amen.

Waiting in a Restaurant

Prayer

O God, you have given to humanity the bounty of your earth and the talent to prepare it to give pleasure. As I wait to be seated or served, help me to reflect on the grace of being in a place where all of your blessings come together in this meal. Amen.

The Word of God

On this mountain the LORD of hosts
will make for all peoples
a feast of rich food, a feast of well-matured wines,
of rich food filled with marrow, of well-aged wines
strained clear.

Isaiah 25:6

Reflection

If you are alone waiting to be seated at your table or alone waiting for your meal, it is a good time to reflect on all the gifts that God has bestowed on humanity that will be represented in the meal that you are anticipating: the fertile fields and abundant crops, the fruitfulness of the beasts of the land, air, and waters, the stewardship of the farmers, ranchers, and fishermen who harvest them.

In order to be served to you, much of this food must be brought to this place by people and technology which has built on generations of progress that comes from talent and ingenuity that can only be a gift from God. And finally, people who share in God's creative work fashion this meal for you, and people who share in God's benevolent deeds serve this meal to you.

A Moment With God

Think about those who made this meal possible.

Lord, bless with your grace the people who produced, transported, are preparing, and will serve this meal.

Reflect on all those for whom a meal like this will never be possible.

Lord, uphold all of those who are hungry and who are working to feed and in all ways improve the lot of those who hunger.

What other prayers do you have at this time?

Prayer

O God, Creator of all things, you are the origin of all that is good in our lives. I pray in humble gratitude for all of the gifts you have bestowed on me. I praise and thank you for this meal, for those who made it possible, and for the company I enjoy. I ask this through Christ our Lord. Amen.

Waiting in Line at the Post Office

Prayer

O Lord, who sent messages to his people by way of angels, be present to me as I run this errand. May the business I have here today at the post office be life-giving to all who are affected by it. Amen.

The Word of God

In the sixth month the angel Gabriel was sent by God to a town in Galilee called Nazareth, to a virgin engaged to a man whose name was Joseph, of the house of David. The virgin's name was Mary. And he came to her and said, "Greetings, favored one! The Lord is with you."

LUKE 1:26–28

Reflection

Oh, that all messages and packages that go through the postal service could be so alive with grace and blessings! Mary was alone, perhaps in prayer, perhaps doing chores when the angel Gabriel appeared to her. She had no expectation of the message she would receive. Yet it changed her life and the life of her fiancé, Joseph, drastically. Ultimately it changed the world.

The letters and packages we send won't have such an impact on the world, but they do have the potential of bring joy, hope, and happiness to the recipients. It might be good to think about the impact of our mailing on the person who receives it.

Life doesn't always allow for peace and love in every missive. However, a conscious effort of compassion and empathy for others can change the world that surrounds you.

A Moment With God

Reflect on the person who will be receiving mail from you soon. Pray for that person.

Lord, bless ____N.____ on this day and on the day that my mail will reach him (her).

If you are not mailing anything but buying stamps or conducting other business, think about how you will approach the person at the window.

Lord, may I be a bright spot in this person's busy day. Grace me with your patience and compassion for this person.

What other prayers do you have at this time?

Prayer

Lord God of hosts, you sent an angel to bring Good News to Mary, the mother of your Son. Enkindle the joy in my heart so I may be a beacon of your Good News to all I meet today. Bless all those who are affected by my business here today. I ask this through your Son, Christ our Lord. Amen.

Waiting in Line to Vote

Prayer

O Lord, you have blessed me by placing me in a nation in which I can exercise my right to vote without fear or caution. Guide me in my choices so that I may be confident that my decisions will benefit all of your people. Amen.

The Word of God

Peter began to speak to them: "I truly understand that God shows no partiality, but in every nation anyone who fears him and does what is right is acceptable to him. You know the message he sent to the people of Israel, preaching peace by Jesus Christ—he is Lord of all."

ACTS 10:34–36

Reflection

The rhetoric has been loud and often angry. Occasionally a candidate will even claim that he or she has been chosen by God to serve in office. But Peter, chosen by God to lead the Church, stated clearly that God is not partial to anyone. All of those people who show respect to God and do the right things are acceptable to him. Think of the implications that Jesus, around whom the Christian faith is centered, preached only peace. How do our candidates measure up to that tenet of our faith?

The Church tells us to follow our own consciences as we make our voting decisions. But our consciences must be "well-formed." We should know the teachings of Scripture and Church tradition, and we must read the signs of the times in order to make our decisions.

We are privileged to live in a country in which we can trust the electoral process. We are obligated to carefully consider our choices for the good of all God's people.

A Moment With God

As you review your slate of candidates, pray for each one.

Lord, bless ____N.____ with the wisdom and right judgment to do your will for my community, state, and nation.

Pray in gratitude for your right to vote.

Lord, I give you praise and thanksgiving for this nation, which gives all of us the right to exercise this duty of our citizenship.

What other prayers do you have at this time?

Prayer

God of power and might, you have bestowed many blessings on our nation. May the decisions I make today be of benefit to all of your creation, in my country, and in the world. I offer this prayer to you in the name of your Son, Jesus Christ our Lord. Amen.

Waiting While Gassing Up the Car

Prayer

Lord God, you created our natural resources and gave humankind the knowledge to develop the technology I am using. As I make this pause in my journey, let me remember your gifts and my responsibility to be a good steward to them. Amen.

The Word of God

The earth is the LORD's and all that is in it,
the world and those who live in it;
for he has founded it on the seas,
and established it on the rivers.
Who shall ascend the hill of the LORD?
And who shall stand in his holy place?
Those who have clean hands and pure hearts,
who do not lift up their souls to what is false,
and do not swear deceitfully.
They will receive blessing from the LORD,
and vindication from the God of their salvation.

PSALM 24:1–6

Reflection

Those who must drive cars for transportation have a love/hate relationship with gasoline. We know we have to buy it, no matter how expensive it is. If we can't ride the train or bus, then we have to spend time alongside a gas pump. We watch the prices judiciously. We'll drive a few more miles to save two cents a gallon.

We are painfully aware that the oil from which gasoline is derived is a nonrenewable resource that despoils the environment in its production and distribution. And that makes us feel guilty.

It is good to reflect on these facts and the fact that God is the creator of our resources and expects that we will use them responsibly. To use a gift of God to destroy what God has made cannot be justified. Being intentional about what we can do to conserve fuel is the beginning of what we must do to secure those "clean hands and pure hearts" we so desire.

A Moment With God

Pray for the earth and the wisdom to preserve it.

Lord, guide humanity as we live on this fragile planet. Give me the wisdom and courage to be a part of the solution.

Pray for safety as you resume your journey.

Lord, protect me and keep me alert and careful as I journey to my destination.

What other prayers do you have at this time?

Prayer

Creator God, you have given us the earth and all that is in it. Bless and sustain my efforts to steward your creation responsibly. Help me as I try to influence others to do the same. I ask this through Jesus, your Son. Amen.

Waiting for Help to Come

Prayer

O God, you are my protection and my strength. Keep me in your care as I wait for the help I need. Calm my anxiety and ease my fears. Amen.

The Word of God

I lift up my eyes to the hills—
from where will my help come?
My help comes from the LORD,
who made heaven and earth.
He will not let your foot be moved;
he who keeps you will not slumber.
He who keeps Israel
will neither slumber nor sleep.
The LORD is your keeper;
the LORD is your shade at your right hand.
The sun shall not strike you by day,
nor the moon by night.
The LORD will keep you from all evil;
he will keep your life.
The LORD will keep
your going out and your coming in
from this time on and forevermore.

PSALM 121

Reflection

This has most likely not been a good day. If it had been, you would not be waiting for help to come. If you have a phone, you have made your calls. If you don't, then all you can do is wait for a Good Samaritan. No matter what situation you are finding yourself in right now, you are dependent on someone else for assistance, and we find that to be very disturbing and humbling.

In this disturbed and humbled state, it is time to turn to God. Making the act of faith that it takes to turn your safety and well-being over to God can empower you to a new confidence. You will no longer imagine the worst or cower in fear. The Lord who made heaven and earth possesses the power to "keep you from all evil" and "keep your life." Fear has no place in that equation.

A Moment With God

Consciously turn over your situation to God.

Lord, I offer you this situation in which I find myself.

Pray for those who are coming to help you.

Lord, bless those who are hurrying to help me.

What other prayers do you have at this time?

Prayer

God of power and might, you are my keeper. I give myself over to you, and with the psalmist I pray that you will keep me from all evil. Calm my soul and help me wait patiently for the help you will send. I ask this through your Son, Jesus Christ our Lord. Amen.

Waiting Out a Storm

Prayer

O Lord, you have the power to calm the storms of this earth and in our heart. Bring this storm to a close so that we may no longer be distressed by its power. Allow us to resume our activities soon. Amen.

The Word of God

We must no longer be children, tossed to and fro and blown about by every wind of doctrine, by people's trickery, by their craftiness in deceitful scheming. But speaking the truth in love, we must grow up in every way into him who is the head, into Christ, from whom the whole body, joined and knitted together by every ligament with which it is equipped, as each part is working properly, promotes the body's growth in building itself up in love.

EPHESIANS 4:14–16

Reflection

Sometimes we love a storm, especially when we don't need to get out in it. We sit at home or in a comfortable place and try not to think about the people who have to be in the elements because of work, the need to be elsewhere, or because they have no shelter.

When we are the ones who have to be out in the storm, however, it is a different story. We are beset by uncertainty. Am I in danger? Is it safe to drive? Should I try to find shelter? When is it going to end?

The Scripture writers, in a time when there was not the technology to predict or protect people from storms, used them as metaphors for the evils and dangers in which the faithful would often find themselves. Today is no different. The words that Paul wrote to the people of Ephesus ring true today. Ours must be a mature faith, and we must not be distracted or taken in by false doctrine, by blustery people who claim to speak for Christ but do not witness to his law of love.

A Moment With God

Pray for the people who have no shelter from this storm.

Lord, watch over and protect those who are homeless or doing their jobs outside.

Pray for the wisdom to discern the teachings of Christ.

Lord, help me to know truth from falsehood. Inspire me to learn more about my faith.

What other prayers do you have at this time?

Prayer

All-powerful God, you are our protector and our guide. Lead us through the storms of life and the winds of change to the safe shelter of the teachings of your Son so that we may be faithful disciples of Jesus Christ our Lord. Amen.

Waiting in Line at the Checkout

Prayer

God of plenty, as I stand here prepared to pay for these items, I ask that you inspire in me the wisdom and discipline to make responsible decisions. Never let me lose sight of what is real and right in my life and in the life of my family, O Lord, because I have been blinded by my desire for what is new and better. Amen.

The Word of God

> *Ho, everyone who thirsts,*
> *come to the waters;*
> *and you that have no money,*
> *come, buy and eat!*
> *Come, buy wine and milk*
> *without money and without price.*
> *Why do you spend your money for that which is not bread,*
> *and your labor for that which does not satisfy?*
> *Listen carefully to me, and eat what is good,*
> *and delight yourselves in rich food.*
> *Incline your ear, and come to me;*
> *listen, so that you may live.*

ISAIAH 55:1–3A

Reflection

In our culture, it is difficult to avoid being swept up in the consumerism that seems to define our public life. We all want to use good judgment when we shop. We attempt to distinguish our wants from our needs. We try to avoid impulse purchases. And we try to pass these values on to our children while their whole environment, their whole social system seems to conspire against our message.

Perhaps heeding the words of Isaiah may help. When we recognize that all that we have that is truly good, truly of value comes from God, when we recall those times when what we bought did not satisfy, we can have more realistic expectations about what we require for a good life.

A Moment With God

Reflect on the items you are buying.

Lord, may these purchases be used to do good in your sight.

Pray for all of those in your community and in our world whose "wants" can never be attained and whose "needs" will never be met.

Lord, guide us in changing the systems that keep people living in poverty.

What other prayers do you have at this time?

Prayer

O God, I thank you for your generosity to my family and me. Grant that we may use your benevolence wisely, always mindful that our blessings originate with you who lives and reigns forever and ever. Amen.

Waiting for Customer Assistance

Prayer

O God, you come to my assistance whenever I call. Help me now as I wait for someone to assist me in solving my problem and work with this person to get good results. Amen.

The Word of God

When the day of Pentecost had come, they were all together in one place. And suddenly from heaven there came a sound like the rush of a violent wind, and it filled the entire house where they were sitting. All of them were filled with the Holy Spirit and began to speak in other languages, as the Spirit gave them ability.
Now there were devout Jews from every nation under heaven living in Jerusalem. And at this sound the crowd gathered and was bewildered, because each one heard them speaking in the native language of each.

Acts 2:1–2, 4–6

Reflection

You've made it through the maze of phone prompts to customer service, and now you're on hold. During this time you may be anxious about a few things. Will the person be able to help me? Where is the person I will be talking to? What is his or her native language? Will I be able to understand this person? How complicated will this be?

In our small world, many of us communicate with people whose first language is not our own. Our ears constantly must adjust to accents in order to do business.

It may be a comfort to know that we are not the first to have that problem. The known world of the first century was also small, not because of technology, but because of geography and trade. The streets of Jerusalem and other cities on trade routes were a cacophony of many languages. But when the Apostles were called to spread the Good News of Jesus Christ, the Spirit gave them the ability to communicate as necessary. With patience and understanding we, too, can gain that ability.

A Moment With God

Pray that you will be able to work with the person who answers your call.

Lord, help me to listen carefully to this person so that we may work together.

Pray for understanding in our small world.

Lord, guide the people of our world in understanding and respect for each other.

What other prayers do you have at this time?

Prayer

Lord of the universe, you have enriched our world with countless cultures and ethnic groups. Free me from fear and help me to embrace all people as your children and my sisters and brothers. I ask this through Jesus Christ, your Son. Amen.

Chapter 5

Events & Recreation

From the rising of the sun to its setting, the name of the LORD is to be praised.

PSALM 113:3

Waiting for the Fish to Bite

Prayer

Creator God, in the beginning you sent your Spirit over the waters to create the earth and all its creatures. Grant me a good day's fishing so that I may enjoy your generous bounty. But if it is not your will for me to catch fish, may I take delight in being a part of this natural world you have created. Amen.

The Word of God

[Jesus said,] "The kingdom of heaven is like a net that was thrown into the sea and caught fish of every kind; when it was full, they drew it ashore, sat down and put the good into baskets but threw out the bad."

MATTHEW 13:47–48

Reflection

Fishing is a lot like life. You cast your line into the mysterious and unknown waters of your future and cannot know what you will bring forth. It may be an unpalatable bottom feeder. It may be too small to be of benefit to your well-being. It may just be weeds. Or something may be nibbling at your bait with no intention of committing itself. On the other hand it may be a magnificent specimen, a blessing you can either keep for all to see or release so another fisher can enjoy it on another day.

Jesus compares God to a fisherman who with joy throws his net into the sea of humanity to see who will join him in his life, the kingdom of God. But everyone is not worthy or ready to be saved, and so hard choices have to be made. What will God discover about you in his net? A bottom feeder? A small fry too immature, unready to be kept? Someone who is just nibbling around the edges refusing to commit to a full life of faith? Or are you a keeper?

A Moment With God

What do you need to do in your life to be the "magnificent specimen" for God?

Lord, guide me in your ways so that I can live a life worthy of being a "keeper."

Is the water in which you are fishing clean? Pray for all who have the responsibility for clean rivers, streams, and lakes.

Lord, it is the responsibility of all of us to care for your creation. Give us the wisdom and determination to be good stewards of your waters.

What other prayers do you have at this time?

Prayer

Fisher God, you have given me all I need to live in the waters of your creation. Bestow your blessings on me as I make my way to the nets of your kingdom. I ask this through Christ our Lord. Amen.

Waiting for Your Teammates to Show Up

Prayer

God of power and might, you have given humankind the gift of competition to test our integrity and to help us to learn to live cooperatively in community. Keep us all in your care so that we may enjoy this game free of injury and animosity. Amen.

The Word of God

Do you not know that in a race the runners all compete, but only one receives the prize? Run in such a way that you may win it. Athletes exercise self-control in all things; they do it to receive a perishable wreath, but we an imperishable one. So I do not run aimlessly, nor do I box as though beating the air; but I punish my body and enslave it, so that after proclaiming to others I myself should not be disqualified.

1 Corinthians 9:24–27

Reflection

Sports is often said to be a metaphor for life. But how often do we stop and think about what that really means? Playing a game is not only about winning any more than going through life is about winning. Whether your sport has multiple players on a team or you are just playing with one other person on your side, you have to repress your individuality in order to cooperate with your teammates and be an effective competitor. If you are playing a singles game, you are still bound by rules that give you boundaries and an identity as a player.

The Apostle Paul used a sports metaphor to encourage the people of Corinth in their new life as Christians. They required self-control, playing by the rules, and keeping their bodies, souls, and minds healthy so that they would be models of Christian virtue to the pagan society around them. Finally, they had to be ever mindful of the good of their Christian community in all of their decisions and behavior if they were to survive to win that imperishable wreath of salvation.

A Moment With God

Ask God to help you in just one area as a team member during this game.

Lord, guide me today as I seek to improve my play by

_____.

Pray that your team and your competitors avoid injury and enjoy this game.

Lord, instill in everyone involved in this competition a sense of joy in the game, and keep everyone safe from injury.

What other prayers do you have at this time?

Prayer

O God, you are the just judge who oversees how I live my life. In this game, and in my life, guide me in my actions and decisions so that I may be a worthy competitor for my teammates and those I am playing. I ask this through Christ our Lord. Amen.

Waiting for Your Walking/Running Partner

Prayer

All-powerful God, you faithfully journey with me throughout my life. Be with my friend and me on our walk/run today. Keep us safe and free from injury. Amen.

The Word of God

The LORD is the everlasting God,
the Creator of the ends of the earth.
He does not faint or grow weary;
his understanding is unsearchable.
He gives power to the faint,
and strengthens the powerless.
Even youths will faint and be weary,
and the young will fall exhausted;
But those who wait for the LORD shall renew their strength,
they shall mount up with wings like eagles,
they shall run and not be weary,
they shall walk and not faint.

ISAIAH 40:28B–31

Reflection

Running and power-walking have much significance in our culture. People engage in these activities to become healthy, to lose weight, to gain stamina, to strengthen their hearts, to release stress, and often just to enjoy the out-of-doors. At the same time, running has become a metaphor for a lot of what is questionable about our culture: workplace competitiveness, keeping up with the Joneses, the avoidance of problems, the fear that someone is always behind us ready to take our jobs or our station in life.

As you run for the physical benefits, reflect on what running might mean to your spiritual well-being. If you find yourself metaphorically running out of ambition or fear, be confident that God will not desert you. God understands your struggles and gives you the will to work them out.

A Moment With God

Are you "running" in any area of your life?

Lord, help me to bring my life into harmony with my Christian values.

Do you have any health concerns related to your running?

Lord, give me the strength to meet my physical challenges and keep me aware of my body so that I do not injure myself during this run.

What other prayers do you have at this time?

Prayer

Everlasting God, you have given us this day, this trail, and the strength to run on it. Bless my partner and me as we conquer the challenges of this run and of our lives. Renew us when we are weary. Strengthen us when we are weak, in life as well as in running. We ask this through your Son, Christ our Lord. Amen.

Waiting in the Deer Stand or Hunting Blind

Prayer

O God, you created the earth and all her creatures. Then you brought forth humanity to steward your creation with care and respect. In granting me a successful hunt, never allow me to lose reverence for your natural world. Amen.

The Word of God

Let them praise the name of the LORD,
for he commanded and they were created.
He established them for ever and ever;
he fixed their bounds, which cannot be passed.
Praise the LORD from the earth,
you sea monsters and all deeps,
fire and hail, snow and frost,
stormy wind fulfilling his command!
Mountains and all hills,
fruit trees and all cedars!
Wild animals and all cattle,
creeping things and flying birds!

PSALM 148:5–10

Reflection

Sitting in a deer stand or a hunting blind in the silence of a cold morning gives rise to a reverence and awe in which it seems we are joined by all of nature. The fields and their grasses, the trees and their branches, the waters and their reeds, the air and its snowfall, all join with our flesh and bone in praise of God's creation.

As we reflect on the role that God gave humans as creation's greatest caregiver, we must also reflect and recognize that humans are creation's greatest enemy as well. Although hunters are leading preservers of our natural resources, it takes constant vigilance and resolve to continue that mission. Before the deer wanders into your view or the birds fly in, take some time to examine your own role as a steward of your natural environment.

A Moment With God

The psalmist commands that all praise God for the gift of creation. As you look around, for what do you want to praise God?

Lord, I praise and thank you for _____.

Pray for the safety of you and your hunting party on this day.

Lord, keep us in your care today. Let no one get careless and negligent as we hunt.

What other prayers do you have at this time?

Prayer

Lord God, creator of heaven and earth, your hand is apparent in the beauty of our surroundings. Thank you for the blessings of this day. May our hunt be successful and may we never forget the source of the birds of the air, the animals who walk the earth, and the humans who are responsible for their well-being. I ask this through Christ our Lord. Amen.

Waiting in Line for a Concert or Play

Prayer

Father in heaven, you bless us with so many gifts that make life good. Thank you for the opportunity to attend this event, a time of entertainment and diversion. Amen.

The Word of God

Above all, clothe yourselves with love, which binds everything together in perfect harmony. And let the peace of Christ rule in your hearts, to which indeed you were called in the one body. And be thankful. Let the word of Christ dwell in you richly; teach and admonish one another in all wisdom; and with gratitude in your hearts sing psalms, hymns, and spiritual songs to God. And whatever you do, in word or deed, do everything in the name of the Lord Jesus, giving thanks to God the Father through him.

COLOSSIANS 3:14–17

Reflection

Actors, musicians, dancers, all artists are blessed to share in the creative activity of our God. Artists must share their talent for it to even be said that they have talent, or they become the tree falling silently in the forest because no one hears. To squander their gifts through disuse is an insult to God, who bequeathed those gifts to them.

This is why we the audience are important. Without the audience to see, hear, laugh, or cry, the talent of the artist does not exist. The audience is essential to the performance.

It is the same in the sacred liturgy. In every faith tradition, in every church, synagogue, and temple, it is the assembled believers who are the primary ministers of worship. Without the faith and participation of the people, there would be no Church. In Catholicism we say that the assembly is the primary symbol of the presence of Christ. They are not mere observers of the liturgy. They are the ministers of the liturgy.

A Moment With God

How does your participation in the entertainment you shall attend reflect on your participation as a worshiper of God?

Lord, may I bring to your worship with my faith community the same enthusiasm and engagement that I bring to this entertainment event.

Hold up the performers of this event in your prayer.

Lord, inspire these performers in their craft as they bring their art to life for us.

What other prayers do you have at this time?

Prayer

Creator God, you have given us music, theater, and the arts to lift our spirits. Be with me as I enjoy this performance, and inspire me to use my talents in my worship of you. For you are Lord forever and ever. Amen.

Waiting for Christmas

Prayer

Lord God, you sent your Son to live among us as a human being. As I anticipate the celebration of Jesus' birth, calm my soul so that, as I join friends and family in all the festivities, I may exhibit the peace that Jesus brought to us. Amen.

The Word of God

Be patient, therefore, beloved, until the coming of the Lord.
The farmer waits for the precious crop from the earth, being
patient with it until it receives the early and the late rains.
You also must be patient. Strengthen your hearts,
for the coming of the Lord is near. Beloved, do not grumble
against one another, so that you may not be judged.

JAMES 5:7–9

Reflection

All during these weeks and, perhaps, months of preparation it seemed as if we were flying toward Christmas and there would never be enough time to get things done. Now Christmas is upon us, all is ready, and in our eagerness to begin the celebration it seems that time has slowed to a crawl and our anxieties have heightened. Ask any child.

Christmas is a time for patience. The Jewish people, God's Chosen, had to patiently await the coming of the Messiah. Mary and Joseph had to patiently await the birth of God's Son. We have to be patient with our children who are dizzy with excitement. And once we get together with our family and its dynamics, our patience is greatly tried.

James was teaching the early Christians to be patient. But they were waiting for the end of the world, the Second Coming. It did not happen, but there is much wisdom in this passage for us when he speaks of patience, the need for us to "strengthen our hearts" and refrain from "grumbling against one another"—good advice for family celebrations!

A Moment With God

Think about those situations in your family that need your prayers.

Lord, bless my family and be with them in their struggles, especially _____.

Pray for all of those who are in need this Christmas.

Lord, take into your tender care all who are homeless, hungry, and frightened this Christmas.

What other prayers do you have at this time?

Prayer

Father Almighty, you gave us Jesus, Mary, and Joseph—the Holy Family—as a model for our families. As we gather together, give us the patience and heartfelt love we need to celebrate well the birth of your Son, Jesus Christ our Lord. Amen.

Waiting for an Important Day in Your Life

Prayer

Lord God, you have given me all that is good in my life. As I anticipate and prepare for this special day, let me be mindful that you are the source of the good that this day will bring. Amen.

The Word of God

This is the day that the LORD has made;
let us rejoice and be glad in it.
Save us, we beseech you, O LORD!
O LORD, we beseech you, give us success!
Blessed is the one who comes in the name of the LORD.
We bless you from the house of the LORD.
The LORD is God,
and he has given us light.
O give thanks to the LORD, for he is good,
for his steadfast love endures for ever.

PSALM 118:24–27A, 29

Reflection

There are so many important days in your life. You can't possibly single out any one of them as more "special" than another. The day you get your driver's license, graduate, marry, welcome a child into your life, send that child out into life, retire—all of these days, and the thousands of days in between, have the potential to change your life profoundly, and they are all "special" to you at the time.

As you prepare for this significant celebration, it is good to remember who made this day. Much of the stress of planning and preparing for that day can be minimized by reflecting on who the day really belongs to and keeping in mind that all that God has made is good, and nothing you can do will ruin it.

A Moment With God

Ask God's guidance in preparing for this day.

Lord, give me a good perspective when planning and preparing for this day.

Lift up in prayer all those who will be celebrating with you.

Lord, bless all those who will be a part of this day. Keep me mindful of the fact that the most important task I have is the one of hospitality to your sons and daughters.

What other prayers do you have at this time?

Prayer

Creator God, you have given us all of our days to celebrate. Inspire me as I prepare for this day. Give all of us who enter into these festivities a successful celebration so that we can rejoice together and give thanks to you forever through Jesus Christ our Lord. Amen.

Chapter 6

Health Happenings

*Do not, O LORD, withhold
your mercy from me;
let your steadfast love and
your faithfulness
keep me safe for ever.*

PSALM 40:11

Waiting for Your Test Results

Prayer

O God, who knows the anxiety in my mind and heart, calm me as I await my test results. Give me the faith to face whatever the future holds with courage and dignity. Amen.

The Word of God

But ask the animals, and they will teach you;
the birds of the air, and they will tell you;
ask the plants of the earth, and they will teach you;
and the fish of the sea will declare to you.
Who among all these does not know
that the hand of the LORD has done this?
In his hand is the life of every living thing
and the breath of every human being.

JOB 12:7–10

Reflection

As we age, one of the most difficult realities to accept is that we are not in control. For most of us that truth becomes apparent when we have a health crisis. Suddenly we—who thought that we would always be able to determine our own fate by making good decisions, following the rules, and living wisely—are at the mercy of our own aging body.

Waiting for news of your test results is a threshold moment. You have stopped at a threshold of your life where you might step through to the relief of good news or you might step through to a life-changing and life-challenging situation. Allow yourself to pause a moment to remind yourself that God is stepping through with you.

A Moment With God

What is your hope for the outcome of your tests?

Lord, give my doctor and me the answer to what is causing my symptoms. Whatever it may be, quiet my anxieties and place your peace in my heart.

What do you want for your medical providers?

Lord, give my doctor and all who are caring for me at this time the grace of compassion and an understanding of the feelings that I am having now.

What other prayers do you have at this time?

Prayer

God of compassion, my life is in your hands. Be with me as I learn the results of these tests. Rejoice with me if the news is good; uphold me in faith if the news is bad. Either way, I trust in the knowledge that you are by my side along with your Son, Jesus Christ, who lives and reigns with you forever and ever. Amen.

Waiting for Surgery or Treatment for Yourself or a Loved One

Prayer

O God, you have the power to heal the anxious heart. Hold me in your tender care as I wait for surgery or treatment to begin. Let me not be overtaken with fear but make me ever mindful of the hope you place before me. Amen.

The Word of God

A great gale arose, and the waves beat into the boat, so that the boat was already being swamped. But he was in the stern, asleep on the cushion; and they woke him up and said to him, "Teacher, do you not care that we are perishing?" He woke up and rebuked the wind, and said to the sea, "Peace! Be still!" Then the wind ceased, and there was a dead calm. He said to them, "Why are you afraid? Have you still no faith?"

MARK 4:37–40

Reflection

Courage is an elusive thing. People like to think of themselves as confident in the face of adversity, able to confront anything that life might throw at them. It often takes your body failing you to realize how vulnerable you are. The thought of surgery, even minor surgery or painful treatments can fill you with apprehension that can interfere with the healing you desperately need.

But how blessed you are! You have faith. You know that Jesus, who can calm the waves of the sea, can calm the tempest in your soul. Jesus, who suffered unimaginable insults to his body, can take on your suffering as his own. You and Jesus can face this crisis together.

A Moment With God

Uphold in prayer all those who will be caring for you or your loved one in this surgery or treatment.

Lord, give these caregivers the compassion, the skills, the wise judgment, and the gentle touch of your healing ministry.

Repeat as a mantra the words of Jesus, and take them into your heart:

Peace! Be still! Peace! Be still!

What other prayers to you have at this time?

Prayer

God of mercy and healing, strengthen and sustain me as I approach this surgery or treatment. Give me courage, give me hope, give me peace. Journey with me throughout this time as I place my life in your loving care and in the hands of your Son, Jesus Christ, who lives and reigns with you forever and ever. Amen.

Waiting in the Emergency Room

Prayer

O God, you are my help and my salvation. Let me feel your presence as I endure the stress of this emergency. Quickly send us the care and healing we need. Amen.

The Word of God

When [Jesus] entered Capernaum, a centurion came to him, appealing to him and saying, "Lord, my servant is lying at home paralyzed, in terrible distress." And Jesus said to him, "I will come and cure him." The centurion answered, "Lord, I am not worthy to have you come under my roof; but only speak the word, and my servant will be healed." When Jesus heard him, he was amazed and said to those who followed him, "Truly I tell you, in no one in Israel have I found such faith. And to the centurion Jesus said, "Go; let it be done for you according to your faith." And the servant was healed in that hour.

MATTHEW 8:5–8, 10, 13

Reflection

You may experience so many emotions when you have to wait in the emergency room, either for yourself or for a loved one: fear, vulnerability, impatience, and finally anger if the wait is extensive. These feelings impact negatively on your health or the health of the patient who is witness to your meltdown.

What is missing from that list of feelings is trust, the confidence in the power of Jesus Christ that the centurion had. Even in his distress over the illness of his servant, this Roman military officer had such a strong faith that he did not want to trouble Jesus by taking him to his house. He knew that Jesus just needed to "speak the word."

Jesus can do the same for you or your loved one, but you must be calm and have quiet confidence in the power of our Lord.

A Moment With God

What do you need from God right now to benefit you or your loved one who is ill?

Lord, help me discern my/our needs at this time and still my emotions so that I can know when you answer my prayer.

Pray for the emergency-room workers who are caring for you and others.

Lord, bless and uphold these people in their mission of healing.

What other prayers do you have at this time?

Prayer

Father, your healing and compassion have no end. Grant me the faith to put my complete trust in you and the grace to recognize your blessings on this day and in these circumstances. I ask this through your Son and our healer, Jesus Christ the Lord. Amen.

Waiting at a Friend or Loved One's Bedside

Prayer

O God, I thank you for the privilege to be here with _____ N. _____ in this time of illness (or injury). I ask you to make me a source of comfort and healing. Guide my words and actions here today. Amen.

The Word of God

Faithful friends are a sturdy shelter:
whoever finds one has found a treasure.
Faithful friends are beyond price;
no amount can balance their worth.
Faithful friends are life-saving medicine;
and those who fear the Lord will find them.

Sirach 6:14–16

Reflection

When sitting at the bedside of someone you love, who matters to you so deeply, you so desperately want to say something or do something that will heal this person. You want to inspire courage, the will to live, the desire to get well.

Often the words do not come and you feel helpless or ineffectual. You may begin to talk of things that seem insignificant to you, and you chastise yourself for being "shallow."

It is important to know that the person you are with does not care what you talk about. Your presence is what is important, the fact that you care and are there as a friend. The wise Sirach said, "Faithful friends are life-saving medicine." Twenty-two hundred years ago, Sirach knew what medicine is just discovering today: the efficacious effect of the support of friends and family on the healing process.

Sirach also tells us that our relationship with the Lord determines our ability to find friendship, for if we have awe and respect for the Lord, we will treat others the same.

A Moment With God

Hold up before God the person you are sitting with.

Lord, I thank your for giving ____N.____ to me as a friend. Heal her and bring her back to us in good health.

Reflect on those friends who are "a sturdy shelter" for you.

Lord, make me worthy of the people who love and care for me.

What other prayers do you have at this time?

Prayer

Father, your Son, Jesus, was a source of comfort and healing to those around him. Inspire me to be like Jesus as I live out my friendship to ____N.____. Bless and strengthen ____N.____ in her illness and bring her to health again in the name of Jesus Christ our Lord. Amen.

Waiting With a Dying Loved One

Prayer

Lord God, you are present here with us as I vigil with
_____N._____ on his journey toward death. Inspire me to speak
to him from my heart, a heart full of your love and mercy.
Amen.

The Word of God

*[Jesus said,] "Do not let your hearts be troubled. Believe
in God, believe also in me. In my Father's house there are
many dwelling-places. If it were not so, would I have told
you that I go to prepare a place for you? And if I go and
prepare a place for you, I will come again and will take
you to myself, so that where I am, there you may be also.
And you know the way to the place where I am going."
Thomas said to him, "Lord, we do not know where you
are going. How can we know the way? Jesus said to him,
"I am the way, and the truth, and the life. No one comes
to the Father except through me."*

JOHN 14:1–6

Reflection

You have been given the honor of being at the deathbed of a loved
one, one of the greatest privileges you can receive. You probably
did not have the opportunity of being with this person at birth into
this world. Being with this person leaving this world and entering
into eternal life is an experience to be treasured.

Our prayer is always for a peaceful death. We want this for
ourselves and those we love—the acceptance that comes of faith

that leads us to look forward to eternal life with Christ and reunion with those who have gone before us.

If that acceptance has not yet come to your loved one, or if you cannot yet accept what is happening, the words of Jesus to his apostles about the many dwelling places in God's kingdom can be a comfort and a way of opening up a discussion about this dying.

A Moment With God

Ask your loved one to pray for you when he enters the presence of God.

Lord, listen to ___N's.___ prayers for us as he dwells in your kingdom.

Pray for those who will mourn ___N's.___ death.

Lord, bring comfort to the family and friends of ___N.___ as he slips from their sight.

What other prayers do you have at this time?

Prayer

Lord God, you are king of heaven and earth. Bless all the friends and family of___N.___who are vigiling with him as he makes this final journey to eternal life in your kingdom. Grant him a peaceful death. Let ___N.___ know that he is surrounded by our love, a love that will never die, even as he leaves our sight. I ask this through your Son, Jesus Christ our Lord. Amen.

Finding Your Hidden Treasure
The Way of Silent Prayer

ISBN: 9780764-820007

The most important journey in life is the journey inward —
to the depths of our own being. It takes us beyond words and
images into silence. We discover an ancient way of finding God
that has almost become lost.

God Is Always There
Psalms for Every Moment

ISBN: 9780764-821585

In *God Is Always There*, the author invites you to experience
the Psalms, viewing them through the theological virtues of
faith, hope, and love. Experience anew these ancient hymns
of lament and praise, and remind yourself that God truly is
always there.

A Worrier's Guide to the Bible
50 Verses to Ease Anxieties

ISBN: 9780764-821639

Author Gary Zimak writes that anxiety can be a blessing.
If you think this sounds just crazy, then this is the book for you.
Consider what the Word of God teaches us on the subject of
worry in times of confusion, despair, doubt, fear, persecution,
sickness, and troubles.

To Order Visit Your Local Bookstore
Call 800-325-9521 • Visit liguori.org

Liguori Publications offers many titles as eBooks through leading distributors
such as Amazon, Barnes & Noble, Kobo, and iTunes.